Little Red Dot

poems by

Rosanne Singer

Finishing Line Press
Georgetown, Kentucky

Little Red Dot

Copyright © 2018 by Rosanne Singer
ISBN 978-1-63534-404-2 First Edition
All rights reserved under International and Pan-American Copyright Conventions. No part of this book may be reproduced in any manner whatsoever without written permission from the publisher, except in the case of brief quotations embodied in critical articles and reviews.

ACKNOWLEDGMENTS

These poems have appeared previously in the following journals:

Inheritance, *Third Wednesday*
Five years later I answer my father's quiz, *Dash*
The Shape of This Girl, *Passager*
On the third shelf of my aunt's library, *Delmarva Review*
Dead Footnote, *Freshwater*
Red Bento Box, *Bluestem*
Flight 370, *Free State Review*
Bertie's Half Hour, *The MacGuffin*
Army Wife with Gurney, *Connecticut River Review*
Sleeping Boy in Detention Center, *Asphodel*
Bad Partner, *Snail Mail Review*
Muerte, *Xanadu*
Fruit Container in the Shape of a Hexagonal Pavilion, *Delmarva Review*

I want to thank my mother who told me to write; my father, who read anything I wanted to share; writing group members Liz, Judy, Anne, Carol P., Carol R., Nancy, Matt, Saundra and Nan who challenged me; my sisters Gina, Deborah, Sandra and Barbara, who may recognize some of my memories; Steve who always provides love and support; and my darling Marie, a fine writer herself.

Publisher: Leah Maines
Editor: Christen Kincaid
Cover Art: Dr. Yang Cai
Author Photo: Steve Mencher
Cover Design: Elizabeth Maines McCleavy

Printed in the USA on acid-free paper.
Order online: www.finishinglinepress.com
also available on amazon.com

Author inquiries and mail orders:
Finishing Line Press
P. O. Box 1626
Georgetown, Kentucky 40324
U. S. A.

Table of Contents

1-2	Inheritance
3	Five years later I answer my father's quiz:
4	The Shape of This Girl
5	Little Red Dot
6	On the third shelf of my aunt's library
7	Feathers
8	The limited courage of mouse-deer
9	In a funk
10	Dead Footnote
11	Red Bento Box
12	Flight 370
13	Mariam at the soccer field
14-15	Bertie's Half Hour
16	The Fighting Season
17	Army Wife with Gurney
18	The kidney that will travel the world
19	We Cool Too (a found poem)
20	Sleeping Boy in Detention Center
21	Bad Partner
22	Muerte
23	The Five Artful Marriages of X and Y
24	Fruit Container in the Shape of a Hexagonal Pavilion
25	After Being Assigned in a Dream to Write an Essay on the Word Climb

Inheritance

*She has her father's hazel eyes,
her mother's unruly auburn hair.*
Relatives love to trace features
as they appear in a family line,
connecting dots against the random
backdrop of space and time.

Shyness reappears through time,
causing a daughter to lower her eyes
as her mother did, not a random
motion, but a trait that like red hair
might define a family line,
become one of its features.

Maybe there are other features,
impossible to see, passed through time.
My teenage mother saw the police line,
then the crushed skull and dead eyes
of her father, his curly red hair
matted with blood. This was not random.

My auburn locks were not random
nor were many other features,
like my tendency to hide behind hair.
From the beginning of my time
I was afraid, as surely as my eyes
were hazel. Did a gene mutate in the line?

My Jewish father stood in the right line,
although it must have seemed random
when other boys like him died. When I,
his two-year-old daughter, was the featured
guest at his office, in another time
and place, they loved my strawberry hair.

I thought they were police, panicked like a hare.
My father held me high down the line
of desks, as I squirmed until the time
was over. Was this guilt random,
or had shame become a feature
to be passed down, along with hazel eyes?

Now it is your time. What is random,
what of our line will show in your features?
You do not have my hair. Is there fear in your eyes?

Five years later I answer my father's quiz:

A three, maybe a four. On a rare day the sun shines
and for no reason it might be a six. Usually the living room ceiling
is my sky and I forget there is a moon. See that nameless woman
dancing to Little Feat? She is not thinking how her knee
is connected to her hip bone.

I guess he knew all this. But he liked his questions
and his traps. If I had answered nine, he would have raised
an eyebrow. A two, he would have nodded wisely. What father
asks his daughter to rank how happy she is with her life?

The Shape of This Girl

Parabola hair like a helmet,
part straight down the middle
as befits a German daughter.
There is left, there is right
There is right, there is wrong
There is black, there is white.

Full moon face and the endless cycle:
Speak up but not with those words,
why are you silent? Speak up
but not with those words. Silence.

The line from the neck
to the waist:
on one side courage, on the other safety.
Be strong, show some spine
but not like the Queens teenager
who dated a black man in 1969.

Hide yourself
in this triangle of a skirt,
like a six-year-old's stick drawing.
Stand up straight, don't come
to the dinner table wearing lip gloss
or eye shadow.

Cylinder legs won't go far
but won't get you lost.
They are solid containers, restrainers
of restless leg syndrome and
any other restlessness you might feel.

Little Red Dot

        could have been my nickname

line up the neighborhood kids

                I was the shortest

     chosen for no team

called Red for my carrot top

          dotting the unruly landscape
with friends and sisters

    afraid to stand out

restless at the same time

            darting from thing to thing

    cat pawing at an ever-shifting laser dot

never getting it, never settled

On the third shelf of my aunt's library

Picture the inch-thick phonebook of a small city,

the single-line entries, the almost-transparent pages.

Is it a myth that a great actor can make you cry

just by reciting names, addresses and numbers?

Now imagine that same book with names and birthdates only.

No one is returning home, no one will make a phone call.

This is the book of my grandmother and her small city

with its clinical name—Convoy 55, June 23, 1943.

Can there be this many pages, this many names?

She is on page 37. I want the tiny type of her name

to be raised, to feel something of someone I could never call.

Instead I read it aloud for the first time. No actor necessary.

Feathers

Three nights running I hear *feathers*.

Not their almost-silent descent

but the word itself. Who has said it

as I drift between sleep and waking?

I admit I listen for messages

or at least a pun. Have I feathered

my nest or boasted a feather in my cap?

Did someone ruffle my feathers?

None of the above. I have never pictured

my parents in feathery angel wings.

After the early morning death of my father

his grandson heard him say, "I feel

so light." Is that the only way?

My human day weighs more than

a sack of potatoes. I thought it had to.

Was someone saying fly?

The limited courage of mouse-deer

Mouse's spooled tail is the history of hiding
in small spaces, the legacy of dirty,
a sentence of death—the return each night
to the cupboard where Leon lived
for a year, both feeding out of sight.
The twitch of deer's white tail is the history
of crouching in woods, surviving on leaves,
fear of the hunted—where Gittl cowered
in 1942, eating berries and roots.
I am a grandchild of skittish animals,
afraid of heights and the stare of crowds.
It is possible to be tightly wound
even in sleep. It is enough that I walk
down the street, show my face.

In a funk

That's what I called you yesterday
(after the cheeriest woman in the neighborhood
asked how I was doing), as if you were sexy.

What *wonderful world* was Armstrong singing about?
Joy is the distance from the oblong pumpkin
on the door stoop to where I stand in the middle

of the street. Laughter is reaching me from
a burned out star. The dog needs me to romp,
my daughter to prop up her wobbling.

I am walking twenty paces behind my intention.
My aunt asked, *What is your passion? Mine is
swimming.* I didn't say, *drowning.*

Dead Footnote

This year my history ripped itself out
by the roots and I wanted to find you—
you who were named after two rivers,
which might explain the headlong rush
of the day we met thirty years ago
and coursed down Baltimore streets,
wafting wisps of pot. Stopping once to hug me,
you called me soft. I was carried along
by your bicycle-wheel legs rolling past
formstone stoops and incense shops, your mouth
spilling plans for walkable cities and us.
Even the train back north couldn't keep up
as your heart hurtled ahead. *Get off the train,*
you said in Philadelphia. Did someone
want me that quickly? Did that happen?

Red Bento Box
    (for a daughter drowned)

What would a sculptor
call my pose? Mother kneeling
at pier's edge? Crouched crone
grieving? For three years I bend
more easily than I stand.

Here is what you used
to love: wafer-thin seaweed,
cucumber sushi,
fermented black beans, old tastes
for a teenage girl's lunch pail.

I sink to my knees,
my offering a red boat
on silent ripples.
No one stares anymore
at my new religion.

Your lunch travels out
then down. Do you reach for it
as I do for you?
Today I put salted fish
for your twentieth birthday.

Flight 370

I was two-thirds through The Life
of Pi over the Bay of Bengal. Sister,
thank you for the recommendation.
Son in Chicago, a question:
Will there be a grandchild?
Perhaps one with your slim build?

I have been a sea tortoise, heavy, plodding
on land, but you would not believe my grace
as I waft and curl with the water snakes
as though they were brothers, my hair lolling
in all directions, black seaweed to feed
a colony. This is easy, not like everything else.

You are smart, your father's son.
No one is at home waiting for me.

Mariam at the soccer field

An American woman paid her daughter
ten dollars for each goal
wore jeans slashed at the knee
packed quartered oranges smothered
in plastic bags for halftime
relaxed in a collapsible chair
from which she sprang like a bullet
to scream *Go Raptors Go Raptors*
yelled *shame* at the referee
when he missed off-sides
dug her nails into the palm of one hand
to stop from yelling again
smiled at me because our daughters
ran like antelope and didn't shy away
from battle, raised an eyebrow
at my silence and ability to stand still
when they tumbled sharp-limbed
onto the hard ground,
graceless as you, brother,
that afternoon when your body jerked
like the Nimba toad eating its prey
and our Liberian field filled in and piled up
with the young bodies of men.

Bertie's Half Hour

*(Brief truce between British and German
soldiers on Christmas 1915 near Laventie, France)*

What we had in common: Christmas,
A few words, homesickness.

Faces no longer blemished, not yet lined.
Alice or Lotte, girls on our minds.

Ill-fitting uniforms—different colors,
We all looked like youngsters.

We took for granted our dependable bodies,
The machine-like way they kept their ease.

Our voices flat, we knew the words
To *Good King Wenceslas.*

The smell of a cigar reminded us of whiskey,
Crackle of a fireplace in January.

We recognized the unyielding cold
Of a gun or a dead mate.

When we shook hands,
We felt the flesh not the muscle.

Both appeared out of winter gray—
The soccer ball, the hundred players.

We sheltered each other,
No one kept score.

Scrambling in snow and slush,
We could have been bear cubs.

An officer's shout, like a portcullis clang,
Dragged us back from play.

Time shrank, time stretched then tore.
That half hour was the best part of a year.

The Fighting Season

April

Empty rooms with taut white sheets wait
7000 miles away. Nurses cut out bunnies.

May

You never think it will be you, even
as shrapnel opens the stomach of your lieutenant.

June

I have been asleep for seven weeks.
Day one I weighed 150, now 105.

July

Nurses listen for my first words, watch
me rediscover my legs. I am their baby boy.

August

What is the word for when you lie on
your back and go through a tube so they can see your brain?

September

If I had it all to do over
I would never have joined. Don't care if the nurses hear.

Army Wife with Gurney

In the gray morning after rain,
the slick road and deserted parking lot
of the hospital wait like an empty stage.
A skinny blonde in full makeup trots on,
as if someone had shouted "Action!"
She is remembering last year at the mall
when her charged gait propelled her store to store,
shrieking with girlfriends. Now she is a sapling
unable to straighten against her husband's gurney,
as if wind were beating her back. She pushes
harder than she ever has to take him from here
to there. Comfortable shoes would help, but once
she slips into them she will become someone else.

The kidney that will travel the world

I picture wings,
tiny suitcase and passport,
a cartoon that would make me laugh
but I don't in the quiet hospital room.
That's not what she means, this older
Marine wife, not prone to sentimentality.
What a young kidney she has now, one
not even old enough to drink, tucked
into her like a child against a mother's back.
She has made promises to it, as
her husband did to her long ago.
I will take care of you,
travel with you to all
the places you
never saw.

We Cool Too (a found poem)

Young homeless
Seven under a freeway bridge

Our camp
is cool. We

even have
a fire. We

cool there. We
have sleeping

bags. We
can get into

the bridge and out
of the wind.

It wasn't that
bad

last night. We
all right.

Sleeping Boy in Detention Center

> *Will you wake him?*
> *No, not I,*
> *For if I do,*
> *He's sure to cry*
>   (From Little Boy Blue, Mother Goose)

You lie bent like a chicken wing,
head and chest on blue sofa,
legs jutting out. I can't see your face
but if you are in here,
something has happened to separate you
from the whole, make even your thick parts
bony. I don't know who you are
when you wake up, but I want to rub your head
as if you are three, and not sixteen.

Someone once painted you
as Sleeping Herd-Boy,
your face pink and round against a haystack,
one hand open to the air, the other closed
down on your knee. How beautiful
to behold anger at rest,
not like the gentle sleep of a girl.
You are the rainstorm on a sunny day
when they say the devil beats his wife.

Somewhere I have seen the two of us,
peasant woman holding a young boy
asleep on her lap, her expression
unsmiling but fond. See,
I don't want to wake up either
from the dream of saving you,
as if all you needed
was a pose or loving gesture
to put you back together.

Bad Partner

You stood still while I writhed in boredom
at the Blue Angels air show in Ypsilanti,

my blind date flat as the field we watched from.
When I lay in a goodbye sweat of lust,

you spun your arms in a whirligig frenzy.
Then there was the summer things fell apart,

and you were the mud I slogged through,
each day a season of pain.

I want to slap your placid face,
but I could sooner tell the Man in the Moon

to wipe off his grin. If the rhythm
of my heart and yours were ever to match,

I could love you. Is it possible you hate me?
I've steamrolled you through every bad week,

never took you seriously. If I screamed,
wept, laughed hysterically, you stayed by me.

You have waited for me to grow up. I've used you badly.
One day, Time, my neglect will tick you off.

Muerte

That night a girl in red coiled her leg
behind the thigh of her partner.

A chanteuse dared white lights to expose
her tears. We sat at the lip of the stage

bathing in heat and wine, picturing
rose between teeth, sheets rustling,

the same sound as leaves back home
letting go. You found us at the bottom

of the world in our room with no phone,
behind a door with three locks.

Why did I imagine you setting out
on foot? You opened your laptop,

waited as words travelled invisible tracks.
A stranger delivered your midnight knock.

The Five Artful Marriages of X and Y

5
Monet couple poised
at the garden gate, Renoir
rowers on the pond,
marsh grasses are our only
impediment. Finally.

4
Let's burn down the house,
start a war Guernica-style.
You—smug sullen bull,
me, open-mouthed horse shrieking
while pieces of home flew off.

3
Why could your brother
not stay upright like Malevich's
Running Man? For years
we were sad, crazy remnants
sleep-walking a ravine's edge.

2
On the single bed
with open book or sipping
automat coffee,
I was Hopper's lone woman.
We did not want the same thing.

1
Companionable day
mutated into flushed night—
Did you know I was
Watts' Orpheus clawing for
someone met too late, then lost?

Fruit Container in the Shape of a Hexagonal Pavilion

Persimmons hide their sour in a Chinese castle,
disguise as ruby globes. I call a fruit bowl a fruit bowl,
let words tell me who I am. When teenage Ignaz
left glass-strewn Frankfurt in 1939 he chose
a poet's name and became my young father.
When I reprimanded my five-year-old daughter
she called 911 for a better life. I use the phone
to make a phone call, wait for a dial tone.
Even my doctor stretches the words of her trade,
writing in my chart under job, *itinerant bard*.
I will start over, a modern-day Adam, renaming
what is flat, mundane. In the beginning
was life, now called circus with bearded lady,
leaps through flaming hoops, cotton candy.

After Being Assigned in a Dream to Write an Essay on the Word Climb

May I choose another word? *Repose* maybe. What can I say about *climb*
that hasn't been said? I will write about why I can't write about *climb*.
All right, **climb**. I wanted to keep crawling. I hated to look down.
I still do. I remember Pollyanna's fall from the roof-tall oak.
My mother's tears. I clung to the inner wall of the Leaning Tower
of Pisa. Whatever I want to see can be seen from the ground.
One day I saw a corporate ladder. No, I'll stay here, thank you.
I'm not opposed to climbing into bed or someone's arms.
As long as he is not on a mountaintop. I'll swoon from love or
comfort but not the vertigo from *climb*. There are peaks and valleys
to flat. But then there's the mind and soul's flatline without *climb*.
Oh no. And these are my 150 words about *climb*. The end.

2017 marked **Rosanne Singer's** 26th year as a teaching artist with the Maryland State Arts Council. As a poet-in-the-schools, she traveled the state to work with elementary and middle school students, designing residencies to enhance curricular learning. She was also part of arts teams working with pediatric patients at Georgetown University Hospital in Washington, DC and with military members and their families at Walter Reed National Military Medical Center in Bethesda, Maryland. Through The International Federation for Biblio/Poetry Therapy, Rosanne is credentialed as a Certified Applied Poetry Facilitator, training she uses in working with community and teacher groups as well as individuals.

Rosanne's poetry appears in literary journals such as *Pinyon, Atlanta Review, Passager, The MacGuffin, Dominion Review, Mangrove and Miramar,* and various collections have been finalists in national poetry contests. Her writing about the arts was published in *Symphony Magazine, The Washington Post* and *Newsday*. She received individual artist grants from the Maryland State Arts Council and the Arts and Humanities Council of Montgomery County, Maryland.

After nearly 30 years in Maryland where she and her husband raised their daughter, Rosanne now resides in northern California.

www.ingramcontent.com/pod-product-compliance
Lightning Source LLC
LaVergne TN
LVHW041519070426
835507LV00012B/1686